# Chimpanzees

Patricia Kendell

HODDER
Wayland

An imprint of Hodder Children's Books

# Chimpanzees   Dolphins   Elephants
# Lions   Polar Bears   Tigers

© 2002 White-Thomson Publishing Ltd

Produced for Hodder Wayland by White-Thomson Publishing Ltd

Editor: Kay Barnham
Designer: Tim Mayer
Consultant: Richard Barnwell, Head of Africa Team, International Programmes, WWF-UK
Language Consultant: Norah Granger, Senior Lecturer in Primary Education at the University of Brighton
Picture research: Shelley Noronha – Glass Onion Pictures

Published in Great Britain in 2002 by Hodder Wayland, an imprint of Hodder Children's Books.

The right of Patricia Kendell to be identified as the author of this Work has been asserted by her in accordance with the Copyright, Designs and Patents Act 1988.

Photograph acknowledgements:
Bruce Coleman 3 (second & third), 4, 9, 15, 17, 24;
FLPA 12 (Minden Pictures), 13 (T Whittaker), 19 (Michael Gore), 3 (fourth), 25 (Jurgen & Christine Sohns), 26 (Brake/Sunset);
NHPA 28 (Martin Harvey), 11, 16, 20 (Steve Robinson), 18 (Nigel J Dennis);
Oxford Scientific Films 5 (Mike Birkhead), 10 (Konrad Wothe), 29 (Clive Bromhall);
Science Photo Library 3 (first), 14, 21 (Tom McHugh), 22 (Tim Davis);
Still Pictures 1, 8, 23, 32 (Michel Gunther), 7 (John Cancalosi), 27 (Paul Harrison);
WWF  D Lawson 6.

British Library Cataloguing in Publication Data
Kendell, Patricia
  Chimpanzee. - (In the wild)
  1. Chimpanzee
  I. Title
  599.8'85

ISBN: 0 7502 3829 1

Printed in Hong Kong by Wing King Tong Co. Ltd

Hodder Children's Books
A division of Hodder Headline Limited
338 Euston Road, London NW1 3BH

Produced in association with WWF-UK.
WWF-UK registered charity number 1081247.
A company limited by guarantee number 4016725.
Panda device © 1986 WWF ® WWF registered trademark owner.

# Contents

Where chimpanzees live    4

Baby chimpanzees    6

Looking after the babies    8

Family life    10

Grooming    12

Growing up    14

Making friends    16

Eating    18

Using tools    20

Rest and sleep    22

Chimpanzees in danger    24

People and chimpanzees    26

Helping chimpanzees to survive    28

Further information    30

Glossary    31

Index    32

# Where chimpanzees live

Chimpanzees live in forests in parts of Africa.

Of all animals, they are the ones most like people.

# Baby chimpanzees

This proud mother is holding her tiny new baby. Baby chimpanzees can do nothing for themselves at first.

They drink milk from their mother and will stay close to her for at least two years.

# Looking after the babies

Chimpanzees look after their babies very well and are very loving. This baby is giving its mother a kiss.

Baby chimpanzees quickly learn how to cling on to their mother's fur. They ride around on their mother's backs until they are older.

# Family life

Chimpanzees live together in **troops**.
The strongest male chimpanzee becomes the leader.

This chimpanzee shows that he is the leader of the troop by acting fiercely to scare away other males.

# Grooming

Chimpanzees **groom** their babies to keep
their fur clean and free from insects.
It is also very comforting.

Adult chimpanzees groom one another too.

# Growing up

Mother chimpanzees teach their babies where to find food and how to make a nest.

These young chimpanzees have found food
that is good to eat.

# Making friends

Young chimpanzees love to play together.
This helps them to grow stronger.

Like people, chimpanzees' faces tell you when they
are angry, sad, excited or frightened. These chimps
look as if they are worried about something.

# Eating

Chimpanzees eat mainly fruit and leaves. But they like insects too and will sometimes kill small animals.

Chimpanzees hunt early in the morning and in the afternoon. This group is moving through the forest looking for food.

# Using tools

Chimpanzees have learned how to use tools. This chimp is hooking **termites** out of the ground with a stick.

Chimpanzees get most of the water they need from juicy fruit. This thirsty chimp is using a leaf to scoop up water.

21

# Rest and sleep

This group is having a rest in the middle of the day.

This chimpanzee has made a nest of branches and leaves, high up in a tree. It will sleep here at night, out of reach of danger.

# Chimpanzees in danger

This chimpanzee is giving the alarm call because there is a leopard nearby.

This mother is protecting her baby from danger.

# People and chimpanzees

Chimpanzees are losing their forest home.
People are cutting down more and more trees
for wood and to make room for crops.

Young chimpanzees are captured and **smuggled** abroad. They are sold as pets, or used for **medical research**.

# Helping chimpanzees to survive

These **orphan** babies have been rescued because they will not survive alone in the wild. Keepers teach them some of the skills they would have learned from their mothers.

These chimpanzees are safe because they live in a part
of the rainforest that has been made into a **wildlife
reserve**. Here, all the trees and animals are protected.

# Further information

Find out more about how we can help chimpanzees in the future.

## ORGANISATIONS TO CONTACT

**WWF-UK**
Panda House, Weyside Park,
Godalming, Surrey GU7 1XR
Tel: 01483 426444
http://www.wwf-uk.org

**The Jane Goodall Institute**
15 Clarendon Park, Lymington,
Hants SO4X 8AX
Tel: 01590 671188
http://www.janegoodall.org

**International Primate Protection League**
116 Judd Street, London
WC1H 9NS
http://www.ippl.org

## BOOKS

**The Chimpanzee Family Book:**
Jane Goodall and Michael Neugebauer,
North South Books 1997.

**Chimpanzees:** Christine Butterworth,
Raintree Steck-Vaughn Publishing 1990.

**Chimpanzees** (Baby Animals series):
Kate Petty, Barrons Juveniles 1992.

**Chimpanzees:** Barbara Taylor Cork,
Franklin Watts 1990.

# Glossary

## WEBSITES

Most young children will need adult help when visiting websites. Those listed have child-friendly pages that could be bookmarked.

http://www.savethechimps.org
The Center for Captive Chimp Care was established by Jane Goodall and Roger Fouts in 1997 to provide a sanctuary for chimpanzees. The website provides facts about chimps and how to adopt orphans.

http://www.panda.org/kids/wildlife
WWF's virtual wildlife pages provide facts about chimpanzees, how their survival is threatened and what can be done about it.

Visit learn.co.uk for more resources.

learn.co.uk
from The Guardian

**groom** – to clean. Chimpanzees pick out dust and insects from each other's fur.

**orphan** – a young animal whose parents have died.

**medical research** – work done by scientists to find cures for disease.

**smuggled** – taken away in secret, often against the law.

**termites** – white ants that eat wood.

**troops** – a group of chimpanzees living together.

**wildlife reserve** – safe places where wild animals can live.

# Index

**B**
baby  6, 8, 9, 25

**D**
danger  23, 25

**F**
faces  17
food  14, 15, 19
forests  4, 19, 26
fruit  18, 21
fur  9, 12

**G**
groom  12, 13
group  19, 22

**H**
hunt  19

**I**
insects  12, 18

**L**
leader  10, 11
leaves  18, 23

**M**
milk  7
mother  6, 7, 8, 9,
  14, 25, 28

**N**
nest  14, 23

**P**
people  5, 17, 26
play  16

**R**
rest  22

**S**
sleep  22, 23

**T**
tools  20
tree  23, 26, 29

**W**
water  21